GERMANY

WITHIN THE BOUNDARIES OF 1937

Scale 1 : 4,000000

Rügen
Stralsund
Greifswald
Usedom
Kolberg
Stolpe
STETTIN
Rega
Havel
Chorin
Oder
Warthe
BERLIN
Potsdam
Spree
Spreewald
Grünberg
Spree
Bober
Oder
Meissen
Görlitz
Leubus
BRESLAU
DRESDEN
Freiberg
Hirschberg
Burkersdorf
berg
Switzerland
Sudetes
Neisse
Neisse

Samland
KÖNIGSBERG
Darkehmen
DANZIG
Rominten Heath
Nogat
Marienburg
Alle
Allenstein
Osterode

Forest
Passau

esgaden

MARIENBURG

STRALSUND

ROSTOCK

CHORIN

BERLIN

DRESDEN

BRESLAU

MUNICH

WARTBURG

GERMANY

Countryside, Cities, Villages and People

24 COLOUR PLATES, 242 FULL-PAGE PHOTOGRAPHS
BY GERMANY'S LEADING PHOTOGRAPHERS

UMSCHAU VERLAG · FRANKFURT AM MAIN

INTRODUCTION BY RUDOLF HAGELSTANGE

PICTURE CAPTIONS BY HARALD BUSCH

29 th EDITION 1972

REPRODUCTION OF THE PICTURES ONLY ALLOWED WITH THE CONSENT
OF THE PHOTOGRAPHERS AND THE PUBLISHER

© 1956 UMSCHAU VERLAG BREIDENSTEIN KG, FRANKFURT AM MAIN

EDITORS: DR. HARALD BUSCH AND DR. H. BREIDENSTEIN (†), FRANKFURT AM MAIN

JACKET DESIGN BY HANS BREIDENSTEIN, FRANKFURT AM MAIN

PRINTED AND BOUND BY BRÖNNERS DRUCKEREI BREIDENSTEIN KG, FRANKFURT AM MAIN

ISBN 3-524-00041-X · PRINTED IN GERMANY

Germany as a Whole

There are many countries in the world and it is only natural for each of us to rate his native land above all others. The Germans, too, like to praise their beautiful homeland. Many visitors from other lands will understand and share these feelings. Germany has always attracted visitors by reason of the diversity of the countryside and by the sympathy, friendliness and hospitality of her people. Enjoying a central position and open to influences from east, west, north and south, the German towns, especially Berlin, offered a second home to many people of other nations. It was and is even today an essential feature of the German character to be open to others.

This is, of course, hardly surprising. Germany grew up into a nation rather late in the day, in face of strong opposition from the separate states, jealously guarding their own individuality. Denmark is nearer to a Schleswiger than Bavaria. A Düsseldorfer finds it more charming to go to Paris over the weekend than to Berlin. And between a vintner of the Moselle and a peasant of the Erzgebirge, the difference of character might easily justify the setting up of a frontier. This very variety, however, which makes it so difficult for Germany to achieve political unity is a source of richness.

Before the end of the Second World War, a war that was so disastrous for Germany, this variety was to be found within a large frame. Today this frame has been hacked to pieces. The terms Silesia and East Prussia are still used, but are they still living conceptions? It is always the East Prussia or the Silesia of the past that is meant. Germany has been torn asunder by the fortunes of war, but surely Germany does not end behind the iron curtain. Surely every German has the right to expect that the two halves will soon be welded together again and that the peoples, different as they are in character, will soon be able to live together in freedom and harmony.

The traveller standing on a peak of the Alps must imagine Germany to be a long staircase gently sloping down to the sea, washing her northern shores. From the Rhine bent near Basle down to the Königssee near Berchtesgaden stretches the mountain barrier between north and south. In the valleys nestle the most charming little towns in S. Germany; the waters of the Bavarian lakes and of Lake Constance wash the foothills of the Alps. This soil nurtures very headstrong people, opposed to all conformity. Their national costumes are not decorative pieces meant to be admired in the wardrobe; they are intended for daily wear. The Sunday morning procession of church-goers in the Black Forest or Upper Bavaria is an unforgettable scene; Shrove Tuesday in the Lake Constance region has unmistakable features. At the most beautiful points of this first "flight of stairs", formed by Black Forest, Swabian Alps and Bavarian Alpine foothills, the old architects built the finest Baroque churches — Birnau, Weingarten, In the Wies or Beuron for instance. In the valleys of the Danube, Lech, Isar, and Inn, however, lying before the next "flight of stairs" formed by the hills of the Palatinate, Spessart, Odenwald, and Franconian Jura, grew up the historical old towns of Ulm, Augsburg, Munich, Regensburg — and Passau, with its southern air, at the junction of the Ilz, Inn, and Danube. For the most part they were fortunate towns. Trade brought along prosperity and good civic sense and benevolent princes used this wealth for the noble end of furthering culture. Cathedrals, houses of nobles and of wealthy citizens, magnificent secular buildings and parks are to be found here; the table is richly laid with well-spiced food and wines and life often bears a direct, racy character. The farther north one goes, the greater the refinement, though the original core is never entirely lost. The Main has been rightly termed the boundary of the south.

III

The triangle formed by Rhine, Danube, and Main is considered to be the treasure-house of the south. Even the larger towns such as Heidelberg, Freiburg, Bamberg and incomparable Würzburg have their self-drawn boundaries and are imbued with individuality and intimacy. Perhaps in no other place is such fullness and complete mastery of form to be found among German architects. Dazzling proof of this can be seen particularly in the small towns: Rothenburg, Dinkelsbühl, Nördlingen, Miltenberg, Schwäbisch Hall and Gmünd. One could wander for weeks up and down this part of the country without ever tiring of this feast for the eye. A sail down the Main, say from Vierzehnheiligen, reveals a romantic, fairy-tale world. And now the mountains taper down still more — Eifel, Siebengebirge, Westerwald, Taunus, Vogelsberg and Rhön, the last "stair" but one — and rivers herald the plain. The Rhine becomes a mighty torrent attracting our attention. It flows through the lovely Rheingau, where the finest wines mature, and cuts its way through the mountains, collecting the waters of the Neckar, Main, Moselle, and Lahn, before heading for ancient Cologne and gay Düsseldorf and the plain of the Lower Rhine. The Weser flows parallel to the Rhine, its banks being lined with attractive little towns strongly imprinted with the North German character, which finally comes into its own behind the last mountain "threshold", the Sauerland, Teutoburg Forest, Weser Hills, Solling and Harz. East of the Weser and west — as far as Soest — the towns of Hildesheim, Brunswick, Celle, and Goslar still bear witness to a proud past.

In the west, the Ruhr district pulsates with new life. Here industry leaves its mark on the landscape. Here in town after town, the glow of blast furnaces lights up the night sky. Here the dark treasures of the earth are brought to light and here lies a great proportion of the nation's wealth. North of Münster, one of the most venerable old towns, the plain begins, stretching as far as the Hanse towns of Bremen, Lübeck and Hamburg, the gateway to the ocean. Schleswig-Holstein juts out beyond the coastline of the North Sea and Baltic, a proud, unyielding, wind-swept land governed by the ebb and flow of the tide. The sea is a wide, rich border.

And now to central Germany. Although scenically it may lack the heroic character of the south it has a charm all of its own: of moderation and intimacy. The softness and harmony of these fir-clad slopes and green valleys rejoice the heart. It is no chance that the noblest minstrels competed on the Wartburg for the laurels of victory; that Luther struggled for expression; that Schiller, the restless Swabian, found peace here and that Goethe, the Frankfurter, made Weimar his adopted home. And when we mention Leipzig and Eisenach, doesn't Bach, the name of Germany's greatest musical genius, ring in our ears like a fugue? The Harz Mountains around the Brocken, the scene of the Witches' Sabbath, might be termed the sister of the "manly" Thuringian Forest. Here was the junction of the medieval highways: it was here that a prince out hunting might hear of his election as King of Germany. These woods are shrouded in a discreet but unmistakable poetry. We have only to look at "Faust" and the "Journey through the Harz". Fertile land lies between these uplands: the "Golden Mead", mythical burial-ground of Barbarossa.

"Saxon Switzerland" is on a grander scale, but despite a modest resemblance to its more imposing namesake, there is no denying its central German character. Anyone who has wandered along the banks of the River Saale knows that apart from the "castles proud and bold", the charm of this part of the country lies in the river meandering past beautiful towns such as Saalfeld, Rudolstadt, Jena, and Naumburg.

Following the course of the Elbe from Wittenberg past Magdeburg and Tangermünde to Wittenberge — the shortest way northwards to the coast —, you will find calm Mecklenburg stretching out as far as the Oder, with Schwerin, Wismar, Rostock, crossed by small lakes and streams. The Mecklenburg lakes are a paradise for fishermen, sparsely populated and therefore all the quieter and more soothing to those in need of a holiday, imbued with a charm all of their own.

The March of Brandenburg with the River Havel and its many lakes, and Frederick the Great's Potsdam, too, form part of the centre: and is there a single Berliner who doesn't appreciate the benefits of this barren land stretching up to the Oder and down to the enchanted stillness of the Spreewald? Today that is all "frontier land" and the sluggish Oder and, beyond Fürstenberg, its tributary the Neisse are "frontier rivers". Let us pause to look over the border at those provinces in which the German feels as completely at home as a Hessian in Hesse, or a Swabian in Swabia. Breslau, hospitable and decorative, is to the Silesian what royal Dresden and "Little Paris" (Leipzig) are to the Saxon. The Silesians are a people of strong emotions, silent, mystic. Industry never got the upper hand in this country, turning its face towards the hills: the Riesengebirge, Eulengebirge, Waldenburger and Glatzer uplands. The Oder was the Silesian's gateway to the world.

It was harder for the Pomeranians, scattered up and down the country. With the exception of Stettin on the western flank and rich, splendid Danzig that didn't strictly belong to Pomerania, there were scarcely any sizeable towns up there. It was farming land with a 190 mile coastline, harbourless except for the old stronghold of Kolberg, but with beautiful forests and fertile soil.

From Pomerania, the road led to East Prussia in closed railway carriages, through the Polish corridor. The East Prussian, like the Silesian, held an outpost; somewhat soberer, more realistic in character than the Silesian, he was no less reliable. Broad as his dialect, he attacked the soil — fertile in the north, but in the southern part, Masuren, marshy and interspersed with lakes and forests; and in the north lay dreaming the Rominter Heide. A rough, beautiful land, loved with an inarticulate love, not unmixed with a little popular self-irony; far from the centre of the Reich, but nevertheless, with its attractive capital Königsberg, birthplace of Kant, an integral part. The E. Prussian coast, with the two great lagoons, the Frische Haff and the Kurische Haff, seems to merge into the sea, a coast of Japanese austerity, a paradise for bird and beast.

The things we build with our hands can mean very much to everyone of us, but they are destructible. A landscape, however, escapes the destructive hand of men. Its character, air, its magic, remain intact. The memory we keep in our hearts is unassailable and indestructible.

And because we know that everything is in flux, that nothing that is divided and bound together by the hand and brain of man is final, we Germans may in all conscience admit that we still love what we have lost and that, in spirit, we are at one with it.

The Germans of today are the citizens of a partitioned country, but still children of Germany, an entity. It is the country of their birth, it may be the land for which they yearn. Here, at the end of this survey, it is fitting that we should evoke the name of the sorely-tried capital. For the fate of Germany is reflected in miniature in the fate of Berlin, and Berlin's struggle to regain her freedom and her longing for unity should serve as an example.

The burden of everyday cares and the unpropitious political scene often take our minds off Germany and her capital as an entity. And so in this volume, the separate halves have been united — an event to which Germans look forward with hope, faith, and love.

Rudolf Hagelstange

LIST OF ILLUSTRATIONS

Schneiders

Beginn einer Deutschlandreise in Bildern: Herbst über dem Karwendelmassiv mit Tiefkar und Wörnerspitze

Starting out on a pictorial trip through Germany:
autumn in the Karwendel Mountains with Tiefkar and Woernerspitze.

Départ pour une visite en Allemagne:
arrière-saison sur les montagnes du Karwendel avec Tiefkar et Woernerspitze.

Metz

Oberstdorf liegt zu Füßen der mächtigen Allgäuer Berge mit dem Kratzer.

Oberstdorf lies at the foot of the impressive Allgäu mountains. In the background: the Kratzer.

Oberstdorf se niche au pied des montagnes impressionnantes de l'Allgäu. Au fond: le Kratzer.

Einödsbach
im Allgäu
(mit der
Trettachspitze),
der südlichste
bewohnte Punkt
Deutschlands.

Einödsbach
in the Allgäu,
the southernmost
inhabited point
of Germany.
In the background:
the Trettachspitze.

Einödsbach
en Allgäu
à l'extrémité
sud de l'Allemagne.
Au fond:
le Trettachspitze.

3   Heimhuber

Arnold

Arnold

Über Füssen am Lech thront das Hohe Schloß,
einst Sommerresidenz der Augsburger Fürstbischöfe.

The Hohe Schloss, once the summer residence of the prince-bishops
of Augsburg, stands above the town of Füssen.

Le Hohe Schloss, ancienne résidence des princes-évêques d'Augsbourg,
domine la ville de Füssen.

Auf schroffem Fels errichtet, erhebt sich Neuschwanstein,
ein steingewordener königlicher Traum vom Mittelalter.

Dramatically perched on a high rock, Neuschwanstein is
a 19th century realisation of a fairy-tale castle.

Neuschwanstein, qui se dresse sur un rocher escarpé,
est un château de fées construit au 19e siècle.

Groth-Schmachtenberger

Unter der Viererspitze im Karwendel stehen die alten Häuser des Geigenbauerdorfes Mittenwald.

Fine old houses in Mittenwald, the old village of violin-makers, lying beneath the Viererspitze.

De belles maisons solides à Mittenwald, vieux village de fabricants de violons, situé à l'ombre du Viererspitze.

Beckert

Der älteste Teil Partenkirchens unter dem Wettersteinmassiv ist der Floriansplatz.

The Floriansplatz is the oldest part of Partenkirchen, at the foot of the Wetterstein.

La Floriansplatz, située au pied du Wetterstein, est la partie la plus vieille de Partenkirchen.

Inmitten der saftigen Wiesen des Allgäus am Fuße der Lechtaler Alpen nahe der Tiroler Grenze liegt der herrliche Weißensee.

The Weissensee is situated at the foot of the Lechtal Alps near the Tyrolean border and surrounded by the rich pastures of the Allgäu.

Au pied des Alpes du Lechtal à la frontière tyrolienne se trouve le Weissensee, environné des prairies verdoyantes de l'Allgäu.

Schneiders

R. Henneberger

Der Chiemsee mit der Insel Frauenwörth und den Alpengipfeln,
von Gstad aus gesehen.

Chiemsee is one of the best-known Bavarian lakes.
The peaceful island of Frauenwörth seen from Gstad.

Chiemsee, un lac très connu de la Bavière.
L'île tranquille de Frauenwörth, vue du village de Gstad.

Zeitz

Reit im Winkl, ein besonders schneesicheres Skiparadies.

Reit im Winkl, a paradise for skiers.

Reit im Winkl, véritable paradis de neige pour les skieurs.

10/11

Metz

Bertram Luftbild

Berchtesgaden – unterhalb des Watzmann – liegt im äußersten Südosten des deutschen Bundesgebietes.

Berchtesgaden lies at the foot of the Watzmann in the south-east corner of Germany.

Berchtesgaden se niche au pied du Watzmann à l'extrémité sud-est de l'Allemagne.

München. Föhnstimmung über den Dächern der Millionenstadt.

Munich. This is the atmosphere when the foehn blows from the Alps.

Munich. Temps de foehn sur la grande metropole, qui compte plus d'un million d'habitants.

Oerter

C. L. Schmitt

Im Garten des weltberühmten Münchner Hofbräuhauses,
das wohl kein Ortsfremder zu besuchen vergißt.

In the garden of the world-famous Munich Hofbräuhaus. No visitor would miss it.

Le jardin du Hofbräuhaus de Munich, place estimée de rencontre.

Blick auf die Türme der Münchener Altstadt:
Alter Peter, Frauenkirche, Rathaus, Heiliggeistkirche.

Munich: view over the towers of the old city.

Munich, vue sur les tours de la ville ancienne.

C. L. Schmitt

Passau. Unter der Feste Oberhaus vereinigen sich die verschiedenfarbigen Wasser
von Ilz, Donau und Inn.

Passau. The differently coloured waters of the Ilz, the Danube, and the Inn
meet beneath the fortress of Oberhaus.

Passau. Au pied de l'Oberhaus se réunissent les eaux multicolores de l'Ilz,
du Danube et de l'Inn.

Wasserburg wird vom Inn fast ganz eingeschlossen.

Wasserburg is almost completely encircled by the River Inn.

La ville de Wasserburg encerclée presque entièrement par l'Inn.

Kreuztor und Frauenkirche der alten Residenz Ingolstadt an der Donau.

The Kreuztor and Frauenkirche of the old Bavarian ducal seat of Ingolstadt on the Danube.

La Kreuztor et la Frauenkirche, symboles de la vieille résidence d'Ingolstadt s/Danube.

18

Schneiders

Die Backsteinkirche St. Martin in Landshut an der Isar überragt die malerischen Giebelhäuser der Hauptstadt des alten Herzogtums Niederbayern.

The brick church of St. Martin towers over the picturesque gabled houses in Landshut, capital of the former duchy of Lower Bavaria on the Isar River.

19

L'église en briques de St Martin domine les pittoresques maisons à pignon de Landshut sur l'Isar, capitale de l'ancien duché de la Basse Bavière.

Metz

Neumeister

Die Rachelkapelle über dem Rachelsee im Naturschutzgebiet
des Bayerischen Waldes.

The Rachelkapelle (Chapel of Rachel) dominates the Rachelsee
in the national park of the "Bavarian Forest".

La chapelle de Rachel (Rachelkapelle) domine le Rachelsee dans le parc national
de la «Forêt Bavaroise».

Burgruine Weißenstein bei Regen am gleichnamigen Flüßchen.

The ruined castle of Weissenstein near Regen, a town on the river
of the same name.

La ruine de Weissenstein près de la ville de Regen sur la rivière
qui porte le même nom.

Wiesner-Bavaria

Kallmünz an der Naab liegt am Ostrand des Fränkischen Jura.

Kallmünz on the River Naab lies at the eastern edge of the Franconian Jura.

Kallmünz sur la Naab est bâtie sur le flanc du Jura franconien.

Burg Randeck im Altmühltal.

The castle of Randeck overlooking the valley of the Altmühl.

Le château fort de Randeck surplombe la vallée de l'Altmühl.

Busch

Schneiders

Augsburg, die traditionsreiche Hauptstadt Oberschwabens.
Blick in die Maximilianstraße, im Hintergrund Rathaus „Perlachturm" und Dom.

Augsburg, the capital of Upper Swabia, is full of traditions.
Maximiliansstrasse with town-hall "Perlachturm" and cathedral as a backdrop.

Augsburg est la vieille capitale de la Haute Souabe. Vue sur la Maximiliansstrasse avec, en arrière-plan, l'hôtel de ville le « Perlachturm » et le cathédrale.

Auch im Rathaus von Memmingen zeigt sich die besondere Kunstbegabung
der Schwaben.

Memmingen town-hall bears witness to the Swabians' remarkable artistic talent.

L'hôtel de ville de Memmingen est témoin du talent artistique des Souabes.

Aufsberg

Saebens

Die mächtige Klosterkirche von Ottobeuren ist die Krone des schwäbischen Barock.

The huge church of Ottobeuren monastery is a gem of Swabian Baroque.

Le vaste monastère d'Ottobeuren est un joyau de l'architecture baroque souabe.

Wiblingen bei Ulm. Die Klosterbibliothek.

Wiblingen near Ulm. The monastery library.

Wiblingen près d'Ulm. La bibliothèque du monastère.

Das Ulmer Münster
besitzt den höchsten
steingemauerten
Turm der Welt
(161 m).

The spire of Ulm
cathedral is the
highest stone-built
structure in the
world (528 ft).

La flèche de la
cathédrale d'Ulm
(161 m.).

Windstoßer

Regensburg.
Vorhalle und Portal
des gotischen Domes
der altehrwürdigen
Donaustadt.

Venerable
Regensburg
on the Danube.
The Gothic portal
of the cathedral.

La vénérable ville
de Ratisbonne
s/Danube.
Portail gothique
de la cathédrale.

Schmidt-Glassner **28**

Der typisch schwäbische Marktplatz in Biberach.

The typically Swabian market place of Biberach.

La place du marché typiquement souabe de Biberach.

Saebens

Das gotische Rathaus des Schwabenstädtchens Waldsee (1426).

The Gothic town-hall of the little Swabian town of Waldsee (1426).

L'hôtel de ville gothique du petit bourg souabe de Waldsee (1426).

31

Busch

Schneiders

Höhepunkte abendländischer Baukunst. Oben: die spätbarocke Wallfahrtskirche „In der Wies" bei Steingaden. Rechts: St. Marien in Neubirnau am Bodensee.

Supreme examples of occidental architecture. Above: the small church "In der Wies" near Steingaden. Right: St. Mary's (18th century) in Neubirnau.

Architecture occidentale à son apogée. En haut: l'église «In der Wies» près de Steingaden. A droite: l'église baroque Ste Marie de Neubirnau.

Blick auf den Bodensee mit Kloster Maurach. Im Hintergrund die Schweizer Alpen.

View of Lake Constance and the monastery of Maurach. In the background, the Swiss Alps.

Vue sur le lac de Constance et le monastère de Maurach. Au fond: les Alpes Suisses.

Lauterwasser

Auf der Meersburg, ihrer Lieblingsstätte, starb die Dichterin Annette von Droste-Hülshoff.

The poetess Annette von Droste-Hülshoff died in Meersburg castle where she had spent part of her life.

Au château de Meersburg vécut et mourut la poétesse Annette von Droste-Hülshoff.

Ott

Lauterwasser

Das alte Konstanz am Bodensee und sein Wahrzeichen, der Münsterturm.

The ancient town of Constance and its cathedral.

La vieille ville de Constance et sa cathédrale.

Hegaulandschaft mit dem Hohentwiel über Singen.

Hegau landscape with Hohentwiel and Singen.

Le paysage d'Hegau avec Hohentwiel et Singen.

Bei Burg Werenwag. Der Durchbruch der Oberen Donau durch die Schwäbische Alb.

Near Werenwag castle. The Upper Danube has cut this gorge through the Swabian Jura.

Gorge près de Werenwag. Le Haut Danube se fraye un chemin à travers le Jura de Souabe.

Holder

Holtmann

Viele Burgen grüßen vom Rande der Schwäbischen Alb weithin ins fruchtbare Unterland. Der Hohenzollern bei Hechingen.
Hohenzollern near Hechingen is one of the many old castles dominating the plain of the River Neckar on the edge of the Swabian Jura.
Hohenzollern, près d'Hechingen, est un des nombreux châteaux qui dominent la plaine du Neckar, dressés sur la crête du Jura de Souabe.

R. Müller

Das Zollernschloß Haigerloch an der Eyach in der Schwäbischen Alb.

The castle of Haigerloch on the Eyach in the Swabian Jura.

Le château d'Haigerloch qui domine l'Eyach dans le Jura de Souabe.

Kleinfeld

Tübingen am Neckar: Hölderlinsturm, Alte Aula der Universität und Turm der Stiftskirche.

In the old university town of Tübingen on the Neckar.

Coin de vieille ville universitaire de Tubingue s/Neckar.

Geißler

Windstoßer

Schneiders

Leuchtender Herbst im Bärental (Schwarzwald).

The Bärental ("Bear Valley") in the Black Forest.

Dans les montagnes de la Forêt-Noire: la «vallée des ours».

Saebens

Schwarzwaldtannen bei Baden-Baden.

Black-Forest fir-trees near Baden-Baden.

Sapins de la Forêt-Noire près de Baden-Baden.

Im Münster
zu Breisach
am Oberrhein
steht einer
der edelsten
spätgotischen
Schreinaltäre.

Beautiful late
Gothic shrine
in Breisach
minster on the
Upper Rhine.

Belle châsse
datant
des dernières
années
de l'époque
gothique dans la
cathédrale
de Breisach.

Der Münsterturm
der Universitätsstadt Freiburg
im Breisgau gilt als
der schönste aller
gotischen Kirchtürme.

The spire of the cathedral
in the university town
of Freiburg is considered
the most beautiful
High Gothic church towers.

La flèche de la cathédrale
de Fribourg en Brisgau est
la plus belle
de l'époque gothique.

Busch

Baden-Baden, mit seinen Kuranlagen, seit langem einer der elegantesten und bekanntesten Badeorte Deutschlands.

Baden-Baden has long been one of Germany's best-known health resorts.

La ville de Bade, avec ses établissements de cure, est depuis longtemps une des villes d'eaux les plus renommées de l'Allemagne.

Pragher

Karlsruhe, die frühere Hauptstadt des Großherzogtums Baden, ist die Pforte zum Schwarzwald. Blick auf das Schloß.

Carlsruhe, the former capital of the grand-duchy of Baden, is the gateway to the Black Forest. The castle.

Carlsruhe, ancienne capitale du grand-duché de Bade, est un point de départ pour visiter la Forêt-Noire. Le château.

Besigheim, die mittelalterliche Stadt am Neckar, liegt inmitten reicher Weinberge und Obstgärten.

The medieval town of Besigheim is situated on the Neckar in a countryside of vine-covered slopes and orchards.

Besigheim, la cité médiévale sur le Neckar, est située parmi vignes et vergers.

Holtmann

Markgröningen. Das altschwäbische Rathaus während des traditionellen Schäferlaufs.

Markgröningen. The old Swabian town-hall during the traditional "Shepherds' Race".

Markgröningen. L'hôtel de ville pendant les fêtes de la «Course des Bergers».

Maulbronn. Die Brunnenkapelle im besterhaltenen Kloster des hohen Mittelalters in Deutschland.

Maulbronn. The fountain inside the best-preserved medieval monastery in Germany.

Maulbronn. La fontaine à l'intérieur du monastère moyenâgeux le mieux conservé d'Allemagne.

Busch

Hirschhorn ist von besonders anmutigem Reiz unter den alten Städten am Neckar.

Hirschhorn, an old township on the Neckar, has a charm all of its own.

Parmi les anciennes bourgades qui bordent le Neckar, Hirschhorn se distingue par sa grâce.

Schwäbisch Gmünd unter dem Rechberg, türmereiche alte Stadt der Goldschmiede.

Multi-towered Schwäbisch Gmünd lying beneath the Rechberg is an old town of goldsmiths.

Schwäbisch Gmünd, vieille ville d'orfèvres, dresse ses tours nombreuses contre le ciel.

Aufsberg

Wie eine feste Burg Gottes ragt das Kloster Groß-Comburg bei Schwäbisch Hall über die liebliche Kocherlandschaft.

The Benedictine monastery of Gross-Comburg near Schwäbisch Hall overlooking the lovely valley of the Kocher.

Le monastère Bénédictin de Gross-Comburg près de Schwäbisch Hall qui commande la belle vallée du Kocher.

Die alte Stadt —
und wie sie heute wächst.
Jahrhunderte hindurch
war innerhalb des Mauerrings
Raum genug für die Bürger
von Nördlingen, das 1215
freie Reichsstadt wurde.
In unseren Tagen nun
fließen die Neubauten ins
umgebende Ries über.

The old town — and its
present-day expansion.
For centuries there had been
room within the town walls
for the citizens of Nördlingen.

La vieille ville — et comme
elle croît aujourd'hui.
Des siècles durant,
il y avait eu assez d'espace,
à l'intérieur du cercle
des murailles, pour les
habitants de Nördlingen.

E. Retzlaff

Schwäbischer Schäfer aus dem Ries.

Shepherd from the Ries district of Swabia.

Pasteur souabe du pays de Ries.

E. Retzlaff

Fränkische Bäuerin aus Effeltrich.
Franconian peasant woman from Effeltrich.
Paysanne franconienne d'Effeltrich.

Jeiter

Aufsberg

Noch immer umgibt mittelalterlicher Zauber das alte Reichsstädtchen Dinkelsbühl. Oben: Aus der Ebene an der Wörnitz erheben sich stolz Mauern und Wehrtürme.
Rechts: Blick auf das Segringer Tor, eines der vier Stadttore, und das Kornhaus (links im Bild).

Dinkelsbühl has preserved its medieval appearance through many centuries. Above: walls and towers near the River Woernitz.
Right: view toward the Segringer Tor, one of the four town gates, and toward the granary (left).

Dinkelsbühl a préservé son apparence médiévale au travers des siècles. En haut: des remparts et des donjons s'élèvent près de la Woernitz.
A droite : vue sur la Segringer Tor, l'une des portes de la ville, et vers la halle à blé (à gauche).

60

St. Georg in Dinkelsbühl
(1448–1492), der ein-
heitlich reifste aller
Hallenkirchenbauten
in Süddeutschland.

St. George's Church
in Dinkelsbühl
(1448–1492) is the most
mature of all buildings
of its type
in Southern Germany.

L'église St Georges à
Dinkelsbühl (1448–1492)
dépasse en hardiesse
de conception tous les
édifices de ce genre
du Sud de l'Allemagne.

Busch

Zisterzienserklosterkirche Heilsbronn. Blick in das Mittelschiff (12. Jahrhundert).
Church of the Cistercian monastery of Heilsbronn. View towards the central aisle (12th century).
L'église du monastère cistercien de Heilsbronn. Vue sur la grande nef (12e siècle).

Bad Mergentheim. Deutschmeisterbrunnen und Schloß des Deutschen Ordens.

Bad Mergentheim. Deutschmeister fountain and castle of the Teutonic Order.

Bad Mergentheim. Fontaine « Deutschmeister » et château de l'Ordre Teutonique.

Rittersaal in Schloß Weikersheim an der Tauber (1605)

Knights' Hall in Weikersheim on the Tauber (1605)

Salle des Chevaliers, Weikersheim sur la Tauber (1605)

Metz

Jeiter

Das Herz Frankens, des Inbegriffs deutscher Romantik, ist Rothenburg ob der Tauber. Oben: Röderbogen und Markusturm. Rechts: der Marktplatz.

Rothenburg on the Tauber, the heart of Franconia, is the epitome of German romanticism. Above: Röder Arch and Marcus Tower. Right: the market place.

Rothenburg s/Tauber. La Franconie réunit tous les sites charmants et romantiques d'Allemagne. En haut: l'arc Röder et la tour St Marc. A droite: la place du marché.

Bayer

Rothenburg ob der Tauber. Links: Aus dem Taubertal gleitet der Blick weit hinauf zu den Mauern und Türmen der Stadt.
Oben: Am Plönlein schaut man auf zwei Stadttore.

Rothenburg on the Tauber. Left: view from the Tauber valley of walls and towers of the town which is full of history.
Above: the Plönlein, with a view towards two of the old town gates.

69 Rothenburg s/Tauber. A gauche: vue sur la vallée de la Tauber avec la ville en arrière-plan. En haut: le Plönlein avec deux des vieilles portes de la ville.

Sulzfeld, eines der alten fränkischen Mainstädtchen, die zugleich Weinbauorte sind.

Sulzfeld, an old Franconian town famous for its wines.

Sulzfeld, l'un des ces vieux villages sur le Main, en Franconie, où l'on cultive aussi la vigne.

70

Busch

Ansbach. Die ehemalige Hofkanzlei (1594), heute Amtsgericht.
Ansbach. The former chancery of the court (1594).
Ansbach. L'ancienne chancellerie de la cour (1594).

Über den Dächern des abendlichen Nürnbergs, der alten deutschen Reichsstadt mit ihren vielen Türmen.

Night falls over Nuremberg, the old German imperial town, with its many towers.

Nuremberg, ancienne ville libre impériale, offre la nuit une image fascinante.

Busch

Nürnberg. Blick von der Burg auf Dürers Wohnhaus am Thiergärtnertor.
Nuremberg. View of Dürer's house at the Thiergärtner Gate, seen from the castle.
Nuremberg. La maison de Dürer près de la Porte Thiergärtner, vue du château.

Nürnberg. Links: die spätgotische Frauenkirche (1350—1358) zur Weihnachtszeit.
Oben: der Chor der Lorenzkirche (1439—1477) mit dem Englischen Gruß von Veit Stoß (1517) und dem Sakramentshaus von Adam Kraft (1493).

Nuremberg. Left: Frauenkirche (Late Gothic, 1350—1358) at Christmas time.
Above: the choir of the Lorenzkirche (1439—1477) decorated by Veit Stoss (Englischer Gruss, 1517) and Adam Kraft (Tabernacle, 1493).

Nuremberg. A gauche: l'église de Notre-Dame à Noël (1350—1358, gothique flamboyant)
En haut: le chœur de la Lorenzkirche (1439—1477), décoré par Veit Stoss (Englischer Gruss, 1517) et Adam Kraft (tabernacle, 1493)

Nördlich Nürnberg liegt Erlangen, bekannt als Schule des Geistes. Das Collegienhaus der Universität.

Well-known as a great centre of learning, Erlangen lies to the north of Nuremberg. Partial view of the university ("Collegienhaus").

Erlangen, au nord de Nuremberg, est bien connu comme grand centre intellectuel. Vue partielle de l'université («Collegienhaus»).

C. L. Schmitt

Bamberg. Über der alten Bischofsstadt ragt der mächtige Dom aus der Zeit der Staufer.

Bamberg. The magnificent cathedral, dating back to the Hohenstaufen days, rises above the old episcopal town.

Bamberg. La cathédrale magnifique datant de la période Hohenstaufen domine la vieille ville épiscopale.

Bambergs Kaiserdom birgt eine
stolze Fülle klassischer
deutscher Plastik, darunter
(links) das Grabmal Heinrichs II.
von Tilman Riemenschneider
und den „Bamberger Reiter"
(um 1235, rechts), das Sinnbild
christlich-abendländischen
Rittertums.

In Bamberg cathedral, a wealth
of classical German art
treasures can be seen, among
them Henry II's tomb (left)
and the "Bamberg Knight"
(1235, right), the greatest
symbol of Christian chivalry
in the Middle Ages.

La cathédrale de Bamberg est
riche en trésors d'art classique,
parmi ceux-ci le tombeau
d'Henri II (à gauche), et le
«Chevalier de Bamberg» (1235,
à droite), sont les témoignages
les plus significatifs de la
chevalerie chrétienne
au moyen âge.

Bayreuth in Oberfranken, die Stadt Richard Wagners, besitzt das besterhaltene Barocktheater Deutschlands.

Bayreuth in Upper Franconia, famous for its Wagner Festival, has the best-preserved Baroque theatre in Germany.

Bayreuth, célèbre par son Festival Richard Wagner, possède le théâtre baroque le mieux conservé de l'Allemagne.

Foto Marburg

Pommersfelden. Das Treppenhaus des bischöflichen Schlosses Weißenstein.

Pommersfelden. Magnificent staircase of Weissenstein castle, a former bishop's palace.

Pommersfelden. L'escalier magnifique de l'ancien palais épiscopal de Weissenstein.

Die Wallfahrtskirche Vierzehnheiligen inmitten des reichen Frankenlandes.

Vierzehnheiligen pilgrimage church amidst the fertile Franconian countryside.

L'église de Vierzehnheiligen dans le paysage fertile franconien.

Die Gartenfront der Würzburger Residenz (1719–1750).

Würzburg Palace. The façade overlooking the park.

Palais de Wurtzbourg: façade donnant sur le parc.

Die Bischöfe von Würzburg, zugleich Herzöge in Franken, besaßen in der Feste Marienberg das wichtigste Bollwerk über dem alten Mainübergang.

The fortress of Marienberg, a mighty bastion at the Main crossing, was the seat of the Prince-Bishops of Würzburg.

Le vaste bastion de Marienberg qui garde le passage du Mein fut la résidence des Princes-Evêques de Wurtzbourg.

84

Busch

85

Wertheim, eines der vielen altfränkischen Städtchen am Main.
Wertheim, one of the many old Franconian townships on the Main.
Wertheim, un des nombreux bourgs franconiens situés le long du Mein.

Busch

Wolff & Tritschler

Das Rathaus von Michelstadt im Odenwald (1484).

The town-hall of Michelstadt in the Odenwald (1484).

L'hôtel de ville de Michelstadt en Odenwald (1484).

Miltenberg am Main. Reiches fränkisches Fachwerk am „Schnatterloch".

Miltenberg on the Main. Fine specimens of Franconian half-timbering.

De belles maisons à colombage franconiennes à Miltenberg.

Göllner   R. Müller

In den sagenumwobenen Wäldern des Spessarts wirkt das Wasserschlößchen
Mespelbrunn wie ein verwunschenes Märchenschloß.

Mespelbrunn, home of many legends, lies in the Spessart woods
like an enchanted fairy-tale castle in a lake.

Dans la Forêt du Spessart, source de tant de légendes, Mespelbrunn,
véritable château de fée, se dresse au milieu d'un lac.

Ein mächtiger Triumphbogen aus der Renaissancezeit grenzt den Ehrenhof
des alten Schlosses Fürstenau im Odenwald wirkungsvoll ein.

A great Renaissance arch leads into the courtyard of the old castle
of Fürstenau in the Odenwald.

Le vieux château de Fürstenau dans l'Odenwald.

Lossen

Lossen

Die alte Universitätsstadt Heidelberg, einst die Residenz der Pfalz,
ist noch heute ein Zentrum des Geisteslebens.

Heidelberg, former seat of the Electors Palatine,
is famous for its university, founded in 1386.

Heidelberg, ancienne résidence des Electeurs Palatins,
célèbre par la vie étudiante de son université fondée en 1386.

Neckarlandschaft bei Zwingenberg.

Typical Neckar landscape near Zwingenberg.

Paysage typique du Neckar près de Zwingenberg.

90/91

Striemann

In der Pfalz ragen die Ruinen vieler Burgen empor. Blick vom Lindelbrunn zum Rödelstein.

Many fine old castles are in the beautiful hills of the Palatinate. View from the castle of Lindelbrunn towards the Rödelstein.

Maint vieux château domine le joli paysage du Palatinat. Le Rödelstein vu du château de Lindelbrunn.

Wentz

Die große Saarschleife bei Mettlach.

The great loop of the River Saar near Mettlach.

La grande boucle formée par la Sarre près de Mettlach.

Häusser

Blick vom Mannheimer Rheinufer auf Ludwigshafen.

View from the Mannheim bank of the Rhine of Ludwigshafen.

Vue pris de la rive de Mannheim du Rhin.

Schlotte-Breidenstein

Frankfurt am Main, die Geburtsstadt Goethes, ist seit jeher ein bedeutender Handelsplatz gewesen. Mainfront mit Rententurm und gotischem Dom.

Frankfurt on the Main, Goethe's birthplace, has been an important trade centre since the Middle Ages. River Main, Rententurm, and Gothic cathedral.

Francfort-sur-le-Main, ville natale de Goethe, est connu pour ses foires depuis le moyen âge. Le Main, la Rententurm et la cathédrale gothique.

Kleinhans

Auf dem Opernplatz, unmittelbar neben der alten Oper, entstand Frankfurts erste „Hochhausfamilie".

Frankfurt's first "family" of tall office buildings was erected close to the old Opera House.

La première «famille de gratte-ciel» a vu le jour place de l'Opéra, tout près de l'ancien Opéra.

96

Busch

Darmstadt. Blick vom Schloß auf Stadtkirche und Rathaus der ehemaligen Residenz

Darmstadt, a former ducal seat: view of the town church and town-hall seen from the c.

Darmstadt, ancienne résidence ducale; l'église et l'hôtel de ville vus du châ

Busch

Krypta des Domes zu Speyer (1. Hälfte 11. Jahrhundert).

Crypt (first half of 11th century) of Speyer cathedral.

Speyer. Crypte de la cathédrale (première moitié du 11e siècle).

Busch

Worms. Der plastisch geformte Dom ist eine Schöpfung aus der Zeit der Stauferkais

Worms cathedral, dating from the days of the Hohenstaufen empero

La cathédrale de Worms qui date de l'époque des Hohenstaufe

Schmidt-Glassner

Der Dom im „Goldenen Mainz" ist der glanzvollste der drei großen Kaiserdome am Rhein.

The cathedral of "Golden Mainz" is the most splendid of the three great imperial cathedrals on the Rhine.

La cathédrale de «Mayence la Dorée» est la plus splendide des trois grandes cathédrales impériales du Rhin.

Busch

Das Mittelschiff der Klosterkirche Eberbach im Rheingau.

Central aisle of the monastery-church Eberbach in Hesse.

Nef de l'église du monastère d'Eberbach, situé dans la Hesse.

Göllner

Das Kurhaus in Wiesbaden, der Landeshauptstadt Hessens.

Wiesbaden (capital of Hesse), the Kurhaus.

Wiesbaden (capitale de l'Hesse). Le casino.

Busch

Der Brunnenhof in Bad Nauheim, dem Herzbad am Taunus.

The Brunnenhof (Fountain Court) in Bad Nauheim, a spa near the Taunus much frequented by sufferers from heart disease.

La Brunnenhof (Cour de la Fontaine) de Bad Nauheim, station thermale située près des montagnes du Taunus.

H. Retzlaff

Dorf Habel in der Rhön, ein rechtes Stück deutscher Heimat.

The village of Habel in the Rhön mountains.

Le village d'Habel situé dans les montagnes du Rhön.

104

Jeiter

Blick auf Fulda mit Michaelskirche und Bonifatius-Dom.
View of Fulda showing St. Michael's church and the cathedral.
Fulda. L'église Saint-Michel et la cathédrale.

Jeiter

Ullstein

Bad Hersfeld. Die Ruine der 1760 zerstörten ottonischen Stiftskirche.

Bad Hersfeld. The fine collegiate church, destroyed in 1760.

Bad Hersfeld. L'église collégiale. De ce monument significatif détruit en 1760, il ne reste que les ruines.

Kassel, Schloß Wilhelmshöhe. Die von Guernieri zwischen 1701 und 1718 erbaute Herkuleskaskade mit Riesenschloß.

Cassel, Schloss Wilhelmshöhe. Hercules cascade with Riesenschloss (giant's castle). Built by Guernieri between 1701 and 1718.

Cassel. Château de Wilhelmshöhe: la cascade d'Hercule et le Riesenschloss (le château des géants), bâtis par Guernieri entre 1701 et 1718.

Schmuck wie Hessens
Volkstrachten sind
seine freundlichen
Fachwerkbauten.
Das Rathaus
auf dem Marktplatz
zu Alsfeld.

Hesse's cheery half-
timbered buildings
are as trim and
neat as the colourful
regional costumes.
Town-hall and
market place in
Alsfeld.

Comme ses habitants
avec leurs costumes
traditionels, la Hesse
se pare de maisons à
colombage. Ici l'hôtel
de ville d'Alsfeld.

Busch

Marburg an der Lahn.
Das Landgrafenschloß
krönt das Gassengewirr
der Universitätsstadt.

The castle of the
landgraves commands
a good view of the
tangled streets in the
university town of
Marburg on the Lahn.

Marburg. Le château
des landgraves domine
les vieilles rues de cette
ville universitaire.

Busch

Schloß Runkel an der Lahn,
eine eindrucksvolle Burgruine aus romanischer Zeit.

Runkel castle on the Lahn,
an impressive ruin in Romanesque style.

Le château de Runkel sur la Lahn,
ruine majestueuse, construit dans le style roman.

Limburg. Der Dom St. Georg über der Lahn ist ein Meisterwerk
aus der alten deutschen Kaiserzeit (1235).

Limburg. St. George's cathedral overlooking the Lahn
is an architectural masterpiece (1235).

Limburg. La cathédrale Saint-Georges qui domine la Lahn est un chef-d'œuvre
du temps des Empereurs germaniques (1235).

Wolff & Tritschler

Oberwesel am Rhein mit der Liebfrauenkirche und der Schönburg.

Oberwesel on the Rhine with the Liebfrauenkirche (Church of Our Lady) and Schönburg Castle.

Oberwesel s/Rhin. La Liebfrauenkirche (Notre-Dame) et le château de Schönburg.

Schneiders

Der Rhein, Deutschlands bedeutendster Fluß, gewinnt seinen romantischen Reiz vor allem durch seine vielen alten Burgen. Burg Gutenfels über dem Weinort Kaub.
The Rhine, Germany's most important river, gains its impressive beauty from its many castles. Gutenfels castle above the wine-growing village of Kaub.

113   Le Rhin, le fleuve le plus important de l'Allemagne,
manifeste son charme romantique surtout par le grand nombre de ses vieux châteaux forts: ici la forteresse de «Gutenfels» dominant le village-vignoble de Kaub.

Rotgans

Die Rheinschleife an der Lorelei (linker Felsen) zeigt besonders deutlich, wie der Fluß seinen Weg in das Schiefergebirge geschnitten hat.

Near the Lorelei Rock (on the left), one is struck by the manner in which the Rhine has eaten its way into the slate mountains.

On est frappé en regardant la manière dont le Rhin s'est frayé un chemin à travers les montagnes près de la Lorelei (à gauche).

114

Jeiter

Aus Zell an der Mosel kommen herrlich mundige Weine.

Zell is situated on the River Moselle, smaller sister of the Rhine.

Zell, situé sur la Moselle, petite sœur du Rhin.

Koblenz. Das „Deutsche Eck" von der Festung Ehrenbreitstein aus.

Koblenz. View from Ehrenbreitstein of the "Deutsches Eck".

Coblence. Le «Deutsches Eck», vu de l'ancienne forteresse d'Ehrenbreitstein.

Moog-Luftbild

Im Jahre 15 vor Christus von den Römern gegründet, ist Trier die älteste Stadt Deutschlands. Blick auf Dom und Liebfrauenkirche.

Founded in 15 B. C. by the Romans, Treves is the oldest German town. View toward the cathedral and Liebfrauenkirche.

Fondée de l'an 15 a. J. C., Trèves est la plus ancienne ville d'Allemagne. Au centre la cathédrale et l'église Notre-Dame.

Wolff & Tritschler

Busch

Die Landschaft der Eifel verbirgt mit ihren Maaren
(Kraterseen) nicht ihre vulkanische Entstehung.

The austere countryside of the Eifel hills
plainly shows their volcanic origin.

Le paysage montagneux de l'Eifel montre
encore son origine volcanique.

Burg Eltz, zwischen Wäldern tief versteckt,
erhebt sich unweit der Mosel über dem Eltzbach.

Eltz Castle hidden away in the forests
overlooks the River Eltzbach near the Moselle.

Le château d'Eltz, perdu parmi des forêts épaisses,
dans la vallée de l'Eltzbach, non loin de la Moselle.

Sander

Blick vom Rolandsbogen auf Siebengebirge mit Drachenfels und Wolkenburg; links der Petersberg.

The Siebengebirge (Seven Hills) with the Drachenfels and Wolkenburg castles; left, the Petersberg seen from Roland's Bow.

La Siebengebirge, dont le Drachenfels, et le château de Wolkenburg; à gauche: le Petersberg vu du Rolandsbogen.

Die Universitätsstadt Bonn wurde vorläufige Hauptstadt der Bundesrepublik Deutschland. Der Plenarsaal des Bundeshauses.

The university town of Bonn has been made provisional capital of the Federal Republic. Full session of the Federal Diet.

La ville universitaire de Bonn est devenue la capitale provisoire de la République Fédérale. Assemblée plénière au parlement.

Aachen. In der unter Karl dem Großen errichteten Pfalzkapelle steht sein Thron, später der Krönungsstuhl aller deutschen Könige.

Aachen. The coronation throne of the German kings and emperors stands in the cathedral founded by Charlemagne.

Aix-la-Chapelle. Le trône qui a servi au couronnement des empereurs allemands dans la cathédrale fondée par Charlemagne.

Wolff & Tritschler

Darstellung Karls des Großen am Marienschrein in Aachen, einer der bedeutendsten Goldschmiedearbeiten des Mittelalters (um 1220).

Charlemagne as portrayed by medieval goldsmiths on the priceless St. Mary's shrine (c. 1220) in Aachen.

Charlemagne, chef-d'œuvre de l'orfèvrerie médiévale ciselé sur la châsse Ste Marie (c. 1220) qui se trouve à Aix-la-Chapelle.

Schneiders

Das Rheinufer in Köln wird von zwei mächtigen Denkmälern
mittelalterlicher Frömmigkeit bestimmt: dem Dom und davor Groß-St.-Martin.

The silhouettes of the cathedral and of St. Martin's,
both monuments to medieval piety, overshadow the Rhine bank at Cologne.

A Cologne, la rive du Rhin est dominée par les silhouettes de la cathédrale
et de l'église St Martin, splendides témoignages de la piété médiévale.

Hallenslebe

Köln. Feierliches Hochamt im Dom (1248—1560, 1842—1880)

Cologne. High mass celebrated in the cathedral (1248—1560, completed 1880)

Cologne. La grand'messe dans la cathédrale (1248—1560, terminée en 1880

Köln. Ausschnitt aus Stephan Lochners Dombild (um 1440).

Cologne. Stephan Lochner's picture in the cathedral (c. 1440, detail).

Cologne. Le tableau de Lochner (c. 1440, détail) dans la cathédrale.

König David. Detail aus dem Schnitzaltar in der Pfarrkirche zu Kalkar (1522).

A detail from the carved altar in Kalkar parish church (1522).

Détail de l'autel sculpté, dans l'église paroissiale de Kalkar (1522).

Siebert

Düsseldorf. Das Alte Rathaus (1573) der Rheinmetropole mit dem Reiterstandbild des Kurfürsten Jan Wellem (1711).

Düsseldorf. The Old Town-Hall (1573) of the Rhine metropolis with the equestrian statue of the Elector Jan Wellem (1711).

Dusseldorf. La statue équestre de l'Electeur Jan Wellem (1711) devant le Vieil Hôtel de Ville (1573) de la métropole rhénane.

Strache

Neuß, Düsseldorf gegenüber gelegen, besitzt den reifsten der rheinischen Dome aus der romanischen Epoche (begonnen 1209).

Neuss opposite Düsseldorf boasts the most mature of Rhenish Romanesque cathedrals (begun 1209).

La cathédrale romane de Neuss, ville située en face de Dusseldorf, dépasse dans sa conception toutes celles de la Rhénanie.

Das moderne Gesicht
des Rheinlands.
August-Thyssen-Haus in
Düsseldorf.

Modern aspects of the Rhineland.
August Thyssen Building
in Düsseldorf.

La Rhénanie moderne.
Le bâtiment August Thyssen
à Dusseldorf.

Dortmund. Die Reinoldi-Kirche
der größten Stadt Westfalens
wurde im 13. Jahrhundert
erbaut. Ihr Turm ist jünger.

Dortmund. The Reinoldi-Kirche
in the largest city of Westphalia
was built as early as in the
13th century.

Dortmund, la plus grande ville
de la Westphalie.
Reinoldi-Kirche bâtie dans le
13e siècle.

131   Schmieding

Presse- und Werbeamt

Ruhrgebiet, wie man es sich vorstellt. Kupferhütte und DEMAG in Duisburg.

How one normally imagines the Ruhr district to be: industrial plants in Duisburg.

La Ruhr comme on se la représente toujours: complexe industriel à Duisburg.

Der Hafen von Duisburg-Ruhrort
ist der größte Binnenhafen des europäischen Kontinents.

The docks of Duisburg-Ruhrort
form the largest inland port in continental Europe.

Duisburg-Ruhrort est le port fluvial le plus important d'Europe.

Hallensleben

Der gleiche „Korb", der die Kohle ans Licht fördert, stellt auch für den Menschen die Verbindung her
zwischen der Welt „über Tage" und dem weit ausgedehnten Bereich seiner Arbeit tief „unter Tage".

The same cage which brings coal to the surface is for the men a connecting link between their world above ground and the wide sphere of their work under ground.

La même corbeille, celle qui sert à monter le charbon au jour sert de moyen de communication entre ceux qui sont en surface, et ceux restés dans la mine.

Bildstelle Essen

Wichtige Stadt im Ruhrgebiet: Essen. Weihnachtszeit am Münster.

Christmas in Essen, an important centre in the Ruhr area.

Scène de Noël à Essen, un des centres les plus importants de la Ruhr.

Saebens

Rotgans

Niederrheinisches Gehöft bei Xanten.

Lower Rhine farmhouse near Xanten.

Ferme typique de la Basse-Rhénanie près de Xanten.

Land am Rheinstrom. In der Ferne Hamborn.

River landscape. In the distance, Hamborn.

Paysage rhénan près de Hamborn.

Bathe

Das berühmte Rathaus zu Münster (um 1335), in dem 1648 ein Teil des Westfälischen Friedens geschlossen wurde.

Münster's famous town-hall (c. 1335) in which part of the Treaty of Westphalia was concluded in 1648.

L'hôtel de ville célèbre de Münster (c. 1335), où fut conclue en 1648 une partie du traité de Westphalie.

Soest. Turm der
Stiftskirche
St. Patroklus.

Soest. The tower
of the collegiate
church of
St. Patroklus.

Soest. Clocher de
l'église collégiale
St Patroklus.

Hallensleben

Im schönen Sauerland. Das Weischedetal.

Beautiful Sauerland. The Weischede valley.

La vallée de la Weischede dans la belle région du Sauerland.

Wasserschloß Gemen bei Borken in Westfalen.

The Westphalian moated castle of Gemen near Borken.

Le château de Gemen près de Borken en Westphalie.

140/141

Hedendorf im Kreis Stade. Das riesige, weithin einsame, heute zum größten
Teil aufgeforstete Gebiet der Lüneburger Heide ist reich an stolzen Gehöften

Hedendorf in the Stade district. The vast, solitary stretches of the
Lüneburg Heath are rich in proud farmsteads.

Hedendorf, district de Stade. Les landes étendues de Lüneburg
sont riches des fermes superbes.

Einer der schönen Bauernhöfe des niedersächsischen Artlandes:
der Hof Meyer zu Wehdel.

One of the beautiful old farmhouses of the Artland
in Lower Saxony: farm "Meyer zu Wehdel".

L'une des belles fermes de la Basse-Saxe: la ferme «Meyer zu Wehdel».

Jeiter

Schloß Hämelschenburg zeigt die Schmuckfreude der Weser-Renaissance.

Hämelschenburg castle is a typically ornate product of the "Weser-Renaissance".

Le château de Hämelschenburg, riche en ornement, est un témoignage frappant typique du style «Renaissance Weser».

144

Jeiter

Das obere Wesertal bei Steinmühle.
The Upper Weser valley near Steinmühle.
La vallée de la Weser près de Steinmühle.

Der Mittelbau des reich verzierten Rathauses zu Schwalenberg
stammt aus dem Jahre 1579.

The central building of the richly ornamented town-hall at
Schwalenberg/Westphalia dates from 1579.

Le centre de l'hôtel de ville de Schwalenberg fut bâti en l'an 1579.

Klaes

Der Engelschor
der herrlichen
Michaeliskirche
(1033)
in Hildesheim.

The famous
Angels' Choir (1033)
of the
Michaeliskirche
(St. Michael's)
at Hildesheim.

Le célèbre
chœur (1033) de la
Michaeliskirche
à Hildesheim.

Hildesheim.
Das unvergessene
Knochenhauer-
Amtshaus (1529).

Hildesheim.
The unforgettable
Knochenhauer-
Amtshaus (1529).

Hildesheim.
Le Knochenhauer-
Amtshaus (1529)
fut totalement
détruit.

Saebens

Sommer
und Winter
im waldreichen
Harzgebirge.

Summer
and winter
in the wooded
Harz mountains.

Scène d'été et
scène d'hiver
dans les
montagnes
boisées du Harz.

Rudolphi

Busch

Goslar. Der Reichsadler auf dem alten Marktbrunnen (14. Jahrh.).

Goslar. The imperial eagle on the old fountain of the market place (14th century).

Goslar. L'aigle impérial couronne la vieille fontaine (14e siècle) au milieu de la place du marché.

Hege

153

Braunschweig. Der bronzene Löwe, den sich Herzog Heinrich von Bayern und Sachsen (1129-1195) setzen ließ.

Brunswick. The bronze lion erected by proud Duke Henry of Bavaria and Saxony (1129-1195).

Brunswick. Le Lion érigé par le fier duc Henri de Bavière et de Saxe (1129-1195).

Landesbildstelle
Niedersachsen

Wagner

Wahrzeichen der niedersächsischen Landeshauptstadt Hannover ist die
spätgotische Marktkirche. Links das Alte Rathaus.

One of the sights of Hanover, capital of Lower Saxony, is its late Gothic
Marktkirche. On the left, the Old Town-Hall.

La Marktkirche, de l'époque gothique, est l'emblème de Hanovre, capitale de la
Basse-Saxe. A gauche le Vieil Hôtel de Ville.

Neben dem alten das neue, moderne Hannover. Bürohochhaus am
Königsworther Platz.

The new and modern Hanover is growing beside the old.
Administration building in the Königsworth Square.

A côté de l'ancienne ville de Hanovre se dresse la nouvelle cité moderne.
Le gratte-ciel administratif de la place Königsworth.

Busch

Saebens

Celle. Buntes Straßenbild in der alten Residenzstadt.

In the colourful old town of Celle.

Vieux quartier plein à Celle.

156/157

Verden, breit an der Aller hingelagert, ist ähnlich Celle ein Zentrum der Pferdezucht und der Reiter.

Verden, stretching out along the Aller, is, like Celle, a centre for riders and horse-breeders.

Verden, blotti sur l'Aller, est comme Celle un centre d'équitation et d'élevage hippique.

Busch

Lüneburg. Die „Laube", der Ratssaal des altehrwürdigen Rathauses.

Lüneburg. The "Laube", council chamber in the historic town-hall.

Lüneburg. La « Laube », chambre du conseil dans l'ancien hôtel de ville.

Busch

Lüneburg. Die breite Marktstraße Am Sand mit der Johanniskirche.
Lüneburg. The vast marketstreet Am Sand and St. John's Church.
Lüneburg. La rue-marché étendue Am Sand et l'église St Jean.

Kerff

C. L. Schmitt

Wienhausen. Der Nonnenchor in der Kirche des Heideklosters
bei Celle (um 1300).

Wienhausen. The "Nuns' Choir" in the church of the convent
near Celle (c. 1300).

«Chœur des Religieuses» dans le convent de Wienhausen,
près de Celle (appr. 1300).

Die Lüneburger Heide. Fast ist es uns, als wehten die Lieder und Geschichten
Hermann Löns' aus dieser Landschaft herüber.

Lüneburg Heath. Birch trees and heather, juniper and ancient sheep-folds typify
the melancholy mood of the largest German heath.

Les bruyères de Lüneburg. Bouleaux, bruyères, genévriers, ainsi que de vieilles
bergeries, relèvent la beauté mélancolique de ces prairies les plus étendues d'Allemagne.

Müller-Brunke

Wenn das Wasser versiegt, wird der Wind ihre Flügel treiben; wenn der Wind nicht geht, wird das Wasser in die Fächer des Rades greifen: Mühle in der Emsniederung.

Mill in the Ems plains which can be driven either by wind or by water.

Moulin dans la plaine de l'Ems. Il doit sa force motrice à deux éléments, le vent et l'eau.

162

Saebens

Deiche schützen das flache deutsche Küstenland im Marschengebiet wie hier an der Unterweser.

The flat German coastal area is protected by dykes. Above: marshy land on the River Weser.

Le littoral bas de la mer du Nord est protégé par des digues. Au-dessus: terrain marécageux traversé par la Basse Weser.

Dodenhoff

Winter im Niederungsgebiet bei Worpswede.

Winter on the plain near Worpswede.

L'hiver sur la plaine près de Worpswede.

Torfkähne auf der Hamme im Teufelsmoor.

Barges loaded with peat sailing down the River Hamme through the Teufelsmoor (Devil's bog).

Des chalands chargés de tourbe remontent la Hamme, en passant par le Teufelsmoor (terrain marécageux)

164/16

Friedvolle Weite der ostfriesischen Marschlandschaft.
Oben: in Küstennähe bei Norden. Rechts: bei Huntorf zwischen Oldenburg und der Weser.

The quiet vastness of East Frisian marshes.
Above: near the coast, not far from Norden. Right: near Huntorf between Oldenburg and the River Weser.

Vue agréable de la région de marécages dans la Frise Orientale.
En haut: à proximité de la côte, près de Norden. A droite: près de Huntorf, entre Oldenburg et la Weser.

Das Watt im Jadebusen vor Dangast.

Shoal-fishing in the Jadebusen near Dangast.

Côte très plate du Jadebusen à proximité de Dangast.

Busch

Borkum. Die Luftaufnahme des sommerlich belebten Strandes zeigt, wie gewaltig die Brandung gegen den Strand rollt.

Borkum Island. Aerial view of the crowded beach in summer.

Borkum. Photo arérienne de la plage animée, en été.

Cekade Luftbild

Sylt. Steilküste am Roten Kliff bei Kampen.

Sylt. At the "Red Cliff", near Kampen.

Sylt. Au «Rote Kliff» près de Kampen.

Schensky

Helgoland. Die Nordspitze der Buntsandsteininsel in der Deutschen Bucht.

The northern tip of Heligoland, a bright red sandstone rock.

L'extrémité nord d'Helgoland, rocher en grès de couleur rouge.

E. Retzlaff

Fischfang auf See ist harte Arbeit und braucht ganze Kerle.

Deep-sea fishing is rough work and requires tough men.

La pêche au long cours a besoin d'hommes tenaces.

Neuharlingersiel, einer der kleinen Hafenorte zwischen Greetsiel und Dagebüll.

Neuharlingersiel, a small coastal harbour between Greetsiel and Dagebüll.

Neuharlingersiel, un des petits ports de pêche entre Greetsiel et Dagebüll.

Das ehrwürdige Rathaus
zu Bremen . . . . . und der
Treffpunkt aller
Kunstfreunde:
die Bremer Böttcherstraße.

Bremen town-hall . . . . . and
the Böttcherstrasse,
where lovers of the fine
arts meet.

L'hôtel de ville de Brême
. . . . . et la Böttcherstrasse,
lieu de rendez-vous des amis
des arts.

← Francke ↑

Hamburgs Binnenalster von der Lombardsbrücke aus.

Hamburg. The Alster side seen from the Lombard Bridge.

Hambourg du côté de l'Alster vu du Pont Lombard.

Hartz

Hamburgs Rathaus (1886-1897) und das Lichtermeer der abendlichen Großstadt.

The Town-Hall of Hamburg (1886-1897) and the lights of this big city.

L'hôtel de ville de Hambourg (1886-1897) et l'océan de lumières de la grande ville.

Lüden

Hartz

Hamburg und sein Hafen sind zu einem Großgebilde eigenen Charakters zusammengewachsen. Oben: das Wahrzeichen der Stadt, der „Michel".
Rechts: St. Pauli-Landungsbrücken.

Hamburg. Town and harbour have grown into one great unit.
Above: the spire of St. Michael's is a well-known silhouette on this city's skyline. Right: landing-places in St. Pauli.

Hambourg. La ville et le port sont soudés pour former un seul et grand ensemble.
En haut: la tour de l'église Saint-Michel est l'emblème de la ville. A droite: les débarcadères de St. Pauli.

Bauer

C. L. Schmitt

Schloß Glücksburg in der Landschaft Angeln liegt an der äußersten Nordgrenze Deutschlands.

Glücksburg castle lies in a region called Anglia on the northernmost border of Germany.

Le château de Glücksburg est situé à l'extrémité nord de l'Allemagne.

Husum. Ein Bild wie aus den Novellen Theodor Storms, der in dieser Stadt geboren wurde.

Quaint old Husum where Theodor Storm, the novelist, was born.

La ville d'Husum où naquit le poète Theodor Storm.

Schneiders

Flensburg, die nördlichste Stadt Deutschlands, dicht an der dänischen Grenze, liegt malerisch an einem Meeresarm, der Flensburger Förde.

Flensburg, lying picturesquely on the Förde sound, close to the Danish frontier is the northernmost town in Germany.

Flensburg, la ville la plus au nord de l'Allemagne, tout près de la frontière Danoise, repose comme par enchantement sur un bras de mer.

Wolff & Tritschler

Fischersiedlung in der Stadt Schleswig.
In the fishermen's quarter of Schleswig.
Vieux pêcheur dans la ville de Schleswig.

Kerff

Friedrichstadt an der Eider, eine niederdeutsche Idylle.

Friedrichstadt on the Eider. An idyllic North German town.

Friedrichstadt sur l'Eider, idylle au nord de l'Allemagne.

184

Schneiders

Aus der „Rosenstadt" Eutin inmitten der schönen Holsteinischen Schweiz.
Eutin, "town of roses", lying in the heart of "Holstein Switzerland".
Eutin, «ville des roses», située en pleine «Suisse d'Holstein».

Die Lübecker Bucht mit Travemünde.

A view of Lübeck Bay with Travemünde.

Vue vers la Baie de Lübeck avec Travemünde.

Deutsche Luftbild

Kiel, Landeshauptstadt von Schleswig-Holstein. Innenstadt zwischen Kleinem Kiel
und Förde. Im Vordergrund Ostseehalle und Rathaus.

Kiel, capital of Schleswig-Holstein. Aerial view.

Kiel, la capitale de Schleswig-Holstein. Vue aérienne.

Nafzger

Busch

Der Bordesholmer Altar (1515-1521) von Hans Brüggemann, heute im Dom zu Schleswig, ist ein Meisterwerk altniederdeutscher Schnitzkunst.

The Bordesholmer altar (1515-1521), now in Schleswig cathedral, is a masterpiece of old N. German carving.

L'autel de Bordesholm (1515-1521), dans la cathédrale de Schleswig, est un chef-d'œuvre de la sculpture allemande nordique.

Windstoßer

Lübeck. Die unverwechselbare Erscheinung des Holstentors (1477) prägt noch heute das Bild des alten „Vororts" der Hanse.

Lübeck: The unique Holsten Gate (1477) still dominates the old part of this Hanseatic town.

Lübeck. La porte Holsten (1477) donne encore de nos jours son cachet au vieux centre hanséatique.

Weniger rauh als ihre Schwester, die Nordsee, bietet sich die Ostsee dar.
Herrliche Buchenwälder reichen oft bis an den steinigen Strand.

Far less wild than her sister, the North Sea, the Baltic offers
a romantic coastline and lovely beech-woods.

Souvent plus calme que sa sœur, la mer du Nord, la mer Baltique
nous dévoile ses côtes romantiques et ses hêtres charmants.

C. L. Schmitt

Schwerin. Das neugotische Schloß der Großherzöge von Mecklenburg.

Schwerin. The imitation Gothic castle of the grand dukes of Mecklenburg.

Schwerin. Le château faux gothique des grands ducs de Mecklembourg.

Strähle

Strähle

Stralsund liegt auf einer Insel im Strelasund. Vorn St. Marien, rechts St. Jakobi, oben die Nikolaikirche.
Stralsund is situated on an island in the Strelasund. In the foreground: St. Marien, right: St. Jakobi, above: the Nikolaikirche.
Stralsund est situé sur une île du Strelasund. Au premier plan: Ste Marie, à droite: St Jakobi, au-dessus: la Nikolaikirche.

Hagemann

Wismar ist eine der schönsten unter den alten Hansestädten der Ostsee. Hafen und St. Marien.

Wismar is one of the most beautiful of the old Hanseatic towns, situated on the Baltic Sea. Harbour and St. Mary's.

Wismar est l'une des anciennes villes de la Hanse. Le port et l'église Ste Marie.

194

Nowak

Zeugnisse der Backsteingotik finden sich überall im deutschen Norden: Stralsund. Rathaus und Nikolaikirche (im Hintergrund).
Examples of brick Gothic are to be found everywhere in the north of Germany: Stralsund. Town-hall and Nikolaikirche (in the background).
On se trouve des exemples de l'architecture gothique en brique partout l'Allemagne du Nord: Stralsund. L'hôtel de ville et Nikolaikirche (à l'arrière-plan).

R. Müller

Kolberg. Als Merkurhaus war dieses barocke Gebäude den Gästen des vielbesuchten Badeortes bekannt.

Kolberg. This baroque building was well-known to visitors of the much frequented spa as the "House of Mercury".

Kolberg. Cet édifice de style Baroque était bien connu des estivants de cette station balnéaire. Ils le nommèrent «Merkurhaus».

Universitätsstadt Greifswald. Der Markt mit der „Dicken Marie", dem Turm der Marienkirche.
Market place in the old university town of Greifswald showing "Big Mary", the huge tower of the Marienkirche.
Place du marché dans la ville universitaire de Greifswald avec le tour de l'église Ste Marie.

Gewande

An einem Seitenarm der Rega liegt urtümlich malerisch das Fischerdörfchen Kamp
mit seinen früher schornsteinlosen Rauchkaten.

Like a picture from olden days: the romantic fishing-village of Kamp
with its "smoking-cottages" which, in former times, had no chimneys.

Image du temps passé: le port de pêche de Kamp nous présente
ses charmantes «fermes fumantes».

Land an der Ostsee . . . Charakteristische Küstenszenerie
Rügen, zwischen Saßnitz und Stubbenkamme

The rocky Baltic coastline on the island of Rüger

Le littoral rocailleux de la Baltique, à Rüger

Zisseler

Stettin an der Oder, einst wichtigster Hafen und die Hauptstadt Pommerns.

Stettin on the Oder, the most important port and former capital of Pomerania.

Stettin s/Oder, port principal et ancienne capitale de la Poméranie.

Plan und Karte

Plan und Karte

Osterode liegt auf einer Insel zwischen Drewenz und Drewenzsee im sogenannten Oberland.

Osterode is situated on an island between River Drewenz and Lake Drewenz in the so-called "Oberland".

Osterode est situé dans une île entre la Drewenz et lac Drewenz dans le soi-disant «Oberland».

Kuhn

Danzig. Jopengasse und Marienkirche der alten deutschen Hansestadt.

Danzig. Jopengasse and the spire of the Marienkirche.

Danzig. La Jopengasse et la flèche de la Marienkirche.

Die Marienburg an der Nogat bei Danzig, von 1309-1427 Sitz der Hochmeister
des Deutschen Ritterordens.

The fortress of Marienburg on the River Nogat near Danzig,
from 1309-1427 the seat of the Grand Master of the Teutonic Order.

La forteresse de Marienburg sur la Nogat près de Danzig
fut entre 1309 et 1427 le siège du Grand-Maître de l'Ordre Teutonique.

Ostpreußen. Der Wachbudenberg an der Samlandküste bei Klein-Kuhren.

The Wachbudenberg in East Prussia near Klein-Kuhren at the Samland coast.

Le Wachbudenberg en Prusse-Orientale près de Klein-Kuhren à la côte de Samland.

Raschdorf

Charakteristisches Fischerdorf am Kurischen Haff: Brandenburg an der Mündung des Frisching.

A typical fishing-village on the Kurisches Haff: Brandenburg, situated at the mouth of the River Frisching.

Un village de pêcheurs typique de la Kurisches Haff (région d'étangs): Brandenburg, situé à l'embouchure du Frisching.

← Plan und Karte ↑

In den Kleinstädten des Nordostens ist das Rathaus oft mitten auf dem quadratischen Marktplatz gelegen.
Links: Darkehmen. Oben: Allenstein.

In the provincial towns of the north-east the town-halls are often situated in the centre of the market place.
Left: Darkehmen. Above: Allenstein.

Dans les petites villes du nord-est on trouve souvent les hôtels de ville situés au milieu de la place du marché.
A gauche: Darkehmen. En haut: Allenstein.

Hartz

Königsberg, eine Gründung des Deutschen Ordens (1255), war Universitätsstadt und ein wichtiger Hafen- und Umschlagplatz. Blick auf Pregelhafen und Schloß.

Königsberg, a foundation of the Teutonic Order, was an important port of transhipment. View towards Pregelhafen and castle.

Königsberg, une fondation de l'Ordre Teutonique était un port de transbordement très important. Vue vers le Pregelhafen et le château.

Burda

Die alte Universitätsstadt Rostock ist heute auf dem besten Wege, sich zum wichtigsten deutschen Ostseehafen zu entwickeln.
Blick vom Turm der Marienkirche auf die Lange Straße und Hafenanlagen.

Rostock, an old university town, is well on the way to developing into one of Germany's largest and most important harbours.
View from the spire of the Marienkirche towards Lange Strasse and docks.

Rostock, ancienne ville universitaire, comptera parmi les ports les plus grands et les plus importants d'Allemagne.
Vue du clocher de la Marienkirche vers la Lange Strasse et le port.

Hartz

Berlin. Die Ruine der Kaiser-Wilhelm-Gedächtniskirche mit dem Neubau
Professor Eiermanns und das Europa-Center bilden heute den Mittelpunkt
Westberliner Lebens.

West-Berlin. The Gedächtniskirche with its modern extension,
designed by Professor Eiermann, and the "Europe Centre"
today represent the heart of the big city.

Berlin-Ouest. La Gedächtniskirche avec son annexe moderne,
œuvre du Prof. Eiermann, et le « Europa-Center » sont aujourd'hui
le cœur de la grande cité.

Eschen

Die Prachtstraße des Berliner Westens, der Kurfürstendamm,
erstrahlt im abendlichen Lichterglanz.

West Berlin's main thoroughfare, the Kurfürstendamm,
with its bright lights at night.

Le boulevard le plus renommé de Berlin-Ouest. Le Kurfürstendamm,
s'habille de lumière dès que la nuit tombe.

Neumeister

Ein neu erstandenes Berlin im Westen wie im Osten der zweigeteilten Stadt. Links: Autobahn-Stadtring in Westberlin. Rechts: die Karl-Marx-Allee in Ostberlin.
Berlin has arisen from the rubble and destruction on both sides of the sector border. Left: an autobahn in West-Berlin. Right: the Karl-Marx-Allee in East-Berlin.
Berlin comme il apparaît aujourd'hui en deçà et au-delà du rideau de fer. A gauche: autoroute-ceinture à Berlin-Ouest. A droite: Karl-Marx-Allee à Berlin-Est.

213

Das Denkmal des Großen Kurfürsten, Friedrich Wilhelm von Brandenburg, 1698 von Andreas Schlüter geschaffen
und wohl das bedeutendste Reiterstandbild des europäischen Barock, steht seit 1952 vor dem Charlottenburger Schloß in Westberlin.

Statue of Friedrich Wilhelm, Grand Elector of Brandenburg, sculpted in 1698 by Andreas Schlüter,
is undoubtedly the most renowned equestrian statue of European Baroque. Since 1952 it has stood in front of the Charlottenburg Palace in West Berlin.

Le monument édifié à la mémoire de Friedrich Wilhelm von Brandenburg, œuvre d'Andreas Schlüter (1698),
est probablement la statue équestre la plus renommée de l'art Baroque en Europe. Elle se trouve depuis 1952 dans le Château de Charlottenburg à Berlin-Ouest.

dpa

Eine Mauer, die eine große Stadt teilt — ein Tor, das kein Tor mehr sein darf: das Brandenburger Tor mit der wiedergeschaffenen Quadriga.

A wall that dissects a huge city — a gate that does not serve as a gate anymore: the Brandenburger Tor with the restored quadriga.

Un mur qui déchire une grande cité — une porte qui ne s'ouvre plus: la Porte de Brandebourg avec sa quadriga reconstruite:

Sanssouci (1747), das Schloß Friedrichs des Großen bei Potsdam.

Sanssouci (1747), Frederick the Great's palace near Potsdam.

Sanssouci (1747), le château de Frédéric le Grand, situé près de Potsdam.

Baur

Der Turm der Potsdamer Garnisonkirche (1732-1735), der das berühmte Glockenspiel barg.

The tower of the Potsdam Garnisonkirche (1732-1735), once famous for its chimes.

Le clocher de la Garnisonkirche (1732-1735) à Potsdam, jadis renommé par son carillon.

Im Spreewald ersetzen vielfach Wasserläufe die Straßen.

Water-courses replace roads in many parts of the Spreewald.

Des cours d'eau remplacent souvent des routes dans la Spreewald.

Schröder

Rupp

Breite Flußläufe, Seen und Kiefernwälder: Märkisches Land. Blaue Havel im Grunewald.

Wide rivers, lakes, and pine-forests characterise the March of Brandenburg. The River Havel in the Grunewald.

Cours d'eau, lacs, bois de pin — tout cela caractérise la Marche de Brandebourg. La rivière Havel.

Chorin in der Mark. Die Klosterkirche (1334) ist ein bedeutendes Werk der norddeutschen Backsteingotik.

Chorin in the March of Brandenburg. The monastic church (1334) is characteristic of North German brick Gothic architecture.

Chorin dans la Marche de Brandebourg. L'église (1334) fait honneur à l'architecture gothique en brique du nord de l'Allemagne.

Deutsche Fotothek

Die Altmark birgt in ihren alten Städten wahre Kleinodien gotischer Sakral- und Wehrarchitektur.
Das Ünglinger Tor in Stendal.

The Altmark (Old March) still preserves, in its old towns, outstanding examples of ecclesiastical and profane architecture from Gothic times.
The Ünglingen Gate at Stendal.

L'Altmark (l'Ancien-Marc) abrite dans ses vieilles villes de vrais trésors en architecture sacrée et militaire:
la porte d'Ünglingen à Stendal.

Baur

Schmidt-Glassner

Wernigerode mit seinem kurz vor 1500 erbauten Rathaus und den hübschen Fachwerkbauten nennt sich gern „die bunte Stadt am Harz".

Wernigerode, with its town-hall built shortly before 1500 and its attractive half-timbered houses, presents a colourful picture amidst the Harz scenery.

Wernigerode avec son Hôtel de Ville bâti peu avant 1500, et ses maisons à colombage charmantes se fait appeler «la ville pimpante du Harz».

Quedlinburg, am Fuße des Harzes gelegen, war einst Hauptsitz der deutschen Kaiser aus sächsischem Haus. Im Hintergrund Stiftskirche (997–1129) und Schloß.

Quedlinburg, in the foothills of the Harz mountains, was a favourite residence of the German emperors. In the background, collegiate church (997–1129) and castle.

Quedlinburg, situé au pied du massif du Harz, était la résidence préférée des empereurs d'Allemagne. A l'arrière-plan: la «Stiftskirche» (997–1129) et le château.

Busch

Magdeburg.
Blick aus dem Chorumgang
des gotischen Domes
nach Westen.

Magdeburg.
View from the choir
of the Gothic cathedral,
containing the remains
of Otto the Great.

Magdeburg.
Vue du chœur
de la cathédrale gothique
dans lequel sont enterrées
les reliques d'Othon
le Grand.

Halberstadt. Vom Domturm
aus gesehen:
die romanische Liebfrauenkirche (12. Jahrh.).

Halberstadt. The beautiful
Romanesque Liebfrauen-
kirche (12th century),
seen from the
cathedral tower.

Halberstadt.
La Liebfrauenkirche,
datant du 12e siècle, vue du
clocher de la cathédrale.

Weimar ist durch Goethe und Schiller zu einem Symbol für ganz Deutschland geworden.
Oben: Goethes Arbeitszimmer im Goethehaus am Frauenplan. Rechts: Schillers Wohnhaus.

Through Goethe and Schiller, Weimar has become a symbol of the true spirit of Germany.
Above: Goethe's study in his house at the Frauenplan. Right: Schiller's house.

Grâce à Goethe et à Schiller, la ville de Weimar est devenue un symbole de l'esprit allemand.
En haut: le cabinet de travail de Goethe dans sa maison. A droite: la maison de Schiller.

Bartcky   Busch

Naumburg genießt Ruhm durch seinen romanischen Dom und dessen lebensgroße Stifterfiguren. Links: Uta. Oben: Wilhelm von Camburg.

Naumburg is famous for its Romanesque cathedral. Statues of the cathedral-founders Uta (left) and Wilhelm von Camburg (above).

Naumburg est célèbre par sa cathédrale romane. Détail du jubé: Uta (à gauche) et Wilhelm von Camburg (en haut), les fondateurs de la cathédrale.

Hallensleben

Hoch über Eisenach blickt die Wartburg, ein Symbol für alle Deutschen, weit ins Thüringer Land. Der äußere der beiden Burghöfe.

The Wartburg, lying above Eisenach, commands a good view of Thuringia. The outer courtyard of the castle with its memories of Luther.

Le château de Wartburg où se réfugia Luther, domine la ville d'Eisenach et le pays aux alentours. La cour extérieure du château.

Erfurt. Dom und Severi-Kirche über den Dächern der einstigen Universitäts- und heutigen Blumenstadt.

The former university town of Erfurt. The cathedral and Severi-Kirche towering over the roofs of the "city of flowers".

Erfurt, ancienne ville universitaire. La cathédrale et la Severi-Kirche qui dominent cette ville de fleurs.

„Über allen Gipfeln ist Ruh' . . ." Im Thüringer Wald entstand dieses Gedicht Goethes.

The wooded hills of Thuringia gave rise to a famous poem by Goethe.

Les collines boisées de la Thuringe ont inspiré un poème célèbre de Goethe.

Aufsberg

233

Mitteldeutsches Land: Blick von der Leuchtenburg ins Saaletal.
Central German landscape: view of the Saale valley taken from Leuchtenburg castle.
Paysage typique de l'Allemagne centrale: la vallée de la Saale vue du château de Leuchtenburg.

R. Müller

Halle an der Saale. Die Marktkirche (1554) der alten Salz- und Universitätsstadt
und das Denkmal des aus Halle stammenden Komponisten Georg Friedrich Händel (1685-1759).

The university town of Halle on the Saale. The Marktkirche (1554) of this old salt-mining town,
and, in front, the monument to George Frederick Händel (1685-1759), a native of Halle.

La ville universitaire de Halle s/Saale. Devant la Marktkirche (1554) de cette vieille ville de salines
se dresse le monument de Georges Frédéric Händel, né à Halle en 1685.

234

Aufsberg

Leipzig. Das Alte Rathaus der großen Universitäts-, Buch- und Messestadt.

The old town-hall of Leipzig, once centre of the German book trade, and famous for its fairs.

Le Vieil Hôtel de Ville de Leipzig, ville des livres et des foires.

Schloß Moritzburg bei Dresden. Seine heutige Gestalt stammt von Matthäus Daniel Pöppelmann,
dem Architekten des Dresdner Zwingers, der um 1725 aus älterem Bestand (1545) für August den Starken dieses Jagdschloß erweiterte.

Moritzburg Castle near Dresden built by Matthäus Daniel Pöppelmann (1662-1736).

Le château de Moritzburg près de Dresde construit par Matthäus Daniel Pöppelmann (1662-1736).

Strähle

Busch

Der Zwinger in Dresden, 1709-1732 für höfische Festaufführungen erbaut (1945 zerstört, jetzt völlig wiederhergestellt),
ist eine der berühmtesten Architekturanlagen der Barockzeit.

The Zwinger in Dresden (1709-1732) built for court festivities, was destroyed in 1945. Reconstruction of this Baroque palace has now been completed.

Le Zwinger à Dresden (1709-1732) destiné aux festins de la cour, fut détruit en 1945. On en a reconstruit un palais baroque des plus gracieux.

Busch

Busch

Der gotische Dom zu Meißen. Innenraum.

The Gothic cathedral of Meissen. Interior.

La cathédrale gothique de Meissen. L'intérieur.

Gewölbe der spätgotischen Hallenkirche St. Anna. Annaberg, Stadt des Silberbergbaus.

Annaberg. Ceiling in the Late Gothic church of St. Anne in this silver-mining town.

Annaberg. Voûte dans l'église Ste Anne de cette vieille ville minière.

In der Sächsischen Schweiz bricht die Elbe durch das Elbsandsteingebirge. Die Bastei.

In "Saxon Switzerland" — the romantic gorge cut by the Elbe through the mountains: the "Bastei".

En «Suisse saxonne», pays où l'Elbe se fraye un chemin à travers les montagnes. Ici les curieuses formations rocheuses de la «Bastille».

Winter im Erzgebirge: die Reihensiedlung Burkersdorf.

Winter time in the Erzgebirge: the small village of Burkersdorf.

Hiver dans l'Erzgebirge: le petit village de Burkersdorf.

Saebens

Schröder

Die „Lauben" in Hirschberg/Schlesien.

Hirschberg. Typical Silesian arcades.

Hirschberg. Ces passages sont caractéristiques de la Silésie.

Görlitz an der Neiße mit der Justitia an seiner alten Rathaustreppe (1537).

Görlitz on the Neisse. The figure of Justice on the old staircase of the town-hall (1537).

Görlitz sur la Neisse: La statue de la Justice qui veille sur le vieil escalier de l'hôtel de ville (1537).

Wolff & Tritschler

ie ehemalige Abtei Leubus war einer der größten Klosterbauten
es deutschen Ostens.

he Abbey of Leubus, previously one of the greatest German monastery
uildings in the east.

ancienne abbaye de Leubus, l'une des fondations allemandes les plus
mportantes de l'Est.

Der Annaberg mit seinem Franziskanerkloster,
eine der höchsten Erhebungen Oberschlesiens (400 m).

The Annaberg (1200 ft.), one of the highest mountains in Upper Silesia,
is crowned by a Franciscan monastery.

L'Annaberg (400 m), l'une des montagnes les plus hautes de la Haute-Silésie,
avec son monastère franciscain.

Schmidt-Glassner

Das Rathaus am Ring zu Breslau, ein besonders schöner Bürgerbau der späten deutschen Gotik.

Breslau town-hall, a specially-built civic building, dating from the Late Gothic period.

L'Hôtel de Ville sur la Place du Marché de Breslau, très bel édifice datant de la fin du gothique allemand.

R. Müller

Neiße in Oberschlesien. Die alte Waage (1604) und der Rathausturm (1499).
Neisse (Upper Silesia). "The Building of the Scales" (1604) and the town-hall tower (1499).
Neisse (Haute-Silésie). La maison des balances (1604) et la tour de l'hôtel de ville (1499).

Windstoßer

Das Riesengebirge. Der „Große Teich", im Hintergrund die Schneekoppe (1603 m).

The "Giant Mountains". The "Grosser Teich", the Schneekoppe Mountain (4810 ft.) in the background.

Les «Monts des Géants». Le «Grosser Teich», à l'arrière-plan la Schneekoppe (1603 m).